The Dialogues of Lewis and Clark:
A Narrative Poem

WILLIAM CLARK   MERIWETHER LEWIS

The Dialogues of Lewis and Clark

A Narrative Poem

Robert Edson Lee

Colorado Associated University Press

Copyright ©1979 by Jeanne DuPlan Lee
Colorado Associated University Press
Boulder, Colorado 80309
International Standard Book Number: 0-87081-124-X
Library of Congress Card Catalog Number: 78-67631
Printed in the United States of America
Designed by Dave Comstock

Text and dust jacket illustrations are by Sergeant Patrick Gass,
member of the Lewis and Clark Expedition, and are reproduced
from *Gass's Journal of the Lewis and Clark Expedition,* edited by
James Kendall Hosmer (Chicago: A. C. McClurg & Co., 1904).
Frontispiece engravings are from *History of the Expedition Under
the Commands of Captains Lewis and Clark* (2 vols.),   by John Bach
McMaster (New York: A. S. Barnes & Co., 1904).

For Paul M. Levitt and Philip F. Gura

Contents

Foreword

When in the summer of 1976 I first began my own exploration of the American West by coming to teach at the University of Colorado at Boulder, one of my first priorities was to visit Professor Robert Edson Lee. I had met him briefly the year before, in the frantic atmosphere of the Modern Language Association Convention in San Francisco. Holding court in one of the suites of the elegant St. Francis Hotel, he had been the picture of urbanity, helping easily and gracefully to calm a bumbling job candidate. My visit to his home in Boulder would, I thought, reinforce my image of the civilized presence I had encountered in San Francisco.

I was in for an interesting surprise; when Lee met me at his door his appearance was transformed. Jeans and an open-necked Western shirt had replaced his tailored suit. Turquoise beads hung round his neck. And most amazing of all to a provincial New Englander, he was wearing tooled and sharply pointed cowboy boots! As we made our way to the backyard patio, he didn't excuse his appearance. He had been traveling all night and had reached home that morning. "Where did you go?" I asked. "I just got back from straddling the headwaters of the Missouri."

I didn't quite know what to make of his comment; but, as I came to know him better, I realized how in my first two meetings with him the touchstone to his character had been revealed. "Straddling the headwaters of the Missouri!" My God, I thought. What for? Quite simply because at that time Lee was putting the finishing touches to his long poem, *The Dialogues of Lewis and Clark,* and had wanted to recapture the excitement felt by Meriwether Lewis when, on August 12, 1805, he had entered this sentence in his journal: "at the distance of 4 miles further the road took us to the most distant fountain of the waters of the Mighty Missouri in surch of which we have spent so many toilsome days and wristless nights." On that warm summer day in Boulder I had discovered that Lee, too, was an explorer; and that the magic of the Western land he inhabited still moved him to profound sympathy.

The saga of Lewis and Clark epitomized to Lee what was finest about the American character. Their expedition had succeeded in mapping the terrain of the new nation's latest acquisition. Moving through a land hardly touched by white men, they named and gave substance to beauties and terrors inconceivable to the Easterners who had sent them on their way. Through courage, wisdom, and stubborn defiance they charted a land mass so enormous that its addition more than doubled the size of the country. Quite simply, Lee was moved by the account of their voyage because they, like the earliest explorers of the New World, had encountered something, in F. Scott Fitzgerald's incomparable phrase, "commensurate to man's capacity for wonder." To President Thomas Jefferson, Lewis and Clark reported that the West was beyond his wildest imaginings.

So I come back to that idea—East and West. The sophisticated Robert Edson Lee in San Francisco; the deeply tanned, Stetson-toting Robert E. of Boulder and places wilder. The contrast always intrigued people, and sometimes amused them. What was behind these

images? How did his collection of American Indian arti-
facts fit into a living room and study filled with
treasures from Europe and from a Fulbright year in
Warsaw? How could a pair of chaps hang in the same
house with a Giacometti sketch or Frank Lloyd Wright
wallpaper? Once again I found the explanation in Lewis
and Clark.

Here an anecdote is instructive. Rummaging
through one of Boston's secondhand bookstores the
summer after I came to Boulder, I found a lovely old
portrait of Lewis, probably engraved not too long after
his travels were completed. I bought it, had it matted,
and sent it to Lee as a gift. His reply put me off a bit:
"What a nice gift! But it's like giving a person exactly
half of a ten dollar bill—valueless without the other
half. Still, I'll treasure it, frame it, and someday find the
missing half." It suddenly became clear: to Lee, Lewis
and Clark were two parts making one whole. Captain
Meriwether Lewis, Jefferson's private secretary, trained
in literature and philosophy as well as in the natural
sciences, an urbane, introspective man whose journal
entries were replete with abstract ideas and philosophi-
cal remarks. Captain William Clark, Indian fighter and
frontiersman, a skilled engineer and scout who knew
how to handle Indians and river-running, matter-of-
fact, even-tempered, and hardly given to flights of
fancy. Lewis and Clark, I realized belatedly, were the
two parts of Lee's personality, just as they were two
parts of an American mind divided between treasured
dream and harsh reality. In forging his narrative of
their excursion, Lee came to terms, not only with an
exciting account of wilderness exploration, but also
with the dual nature of the American people, of which
his own character was a prime example. In his own per-
sonality, Lee brought together Lewis and Clark, East
and West, civilization and frontier, dream and reality.
The Dialogues is the moving record of that conjunction.

In this poem, through a fusion of fact and imagina-
tion, Lee artistically renders the meaning of Lewis and

Clark's voyage. That he was successful is attested to by the warm receptions always given him when he read from *The Dialogues* in public. Let me mention just one example. In April of 1977, Lee and I traveled to one of the frontiers of Colorado—to the isolated town of Rangely, near Dinosaur National Monument—and read parts of the poem to students and faculty at Colorado Northwestern College. Even today the landscape around Rangely is rugged and wild, with harsh flat expanses broken by sharp mesas, an extraordinary land of wind and light. As we prepared to read, Lee suddenly paused and stared out the window at a remarkable sunset behind one of the mesas. "Isn't that gorgeous?" he asked, and fifty students turned to look with him; from that moment they began to see as he had when he worked on the poem. Rapport was established, and as we went through the reading everyone in the room knew that the author had experienced what Lewis and Clark must have experienced as they viewed a landscape unchanged since the discovery of the continent.

But how was this poem made, and what makes it so special to all those who have heard it read? I suspect the secret lies in the organizing intelligence Lee brought to his task. Obsessed by the idea of writing a long poem about the expedition, he gave years of study to Lewis and Clark's original journals before finally deciding to incorporate into his work significant excerpts from the daily entries of both explorers. It was, I think, at this point that the idea of the "dialogue" emerged, for anyone studying the journals with care quickly realizes the differences between the two men. Lewis the reflective thinker and Clark the earthy pragmatist embody the qualities that animated the people who settled this land. In the contrapuntal verses of his poem, Lee vividly captures the contradictions, and the synthesis, both of which continue to characterize the American people.

Lee offers readers—in his own words and in the accounts of his two heroes—a condensed version of that epic voyage to the Pacific. *The Dialogues* is a compressed poetic sequence that captures the symbolic drama implicit in Lewis and Clark's achievement. The poem most reminds me of Robert Penn Warren's beautiful verse narrative, *Audubon: A Vision,* an attempt to distill poetry from the journals of one of America's premier naturalists. The assumption of both Lee and Warren is that in American history we have first-hand narratives that almost burst into poetry because of their subject matter. All they need to turn them into art is a controlling intelligence, a poetic mind which, by clever and judicious editing and emendation, weaves their raw material into a memorable tapestry. Our history, Lee tells us, *is* poetic; we *are* of epic dimensions, and men like Lewis and Clark, and Audubon, epitomize our grandeur.

Finally, it is worth saying that what seems to me best in this poem is Lee's ability to convey what D. H. Lawrence termed "the spirit of the place." Lee believed in the force of geography; and so do I. Standing once on the headlands at Halibut Point, Cape Ann, Massachusetts, an outcropping of worn granite that might well have been the first land seen by the early Puritan settlers, I suddenly had a vision, a dream-like realization of how it must have felt to see this severe land from that unfriendly water, after so long a crossing. In a sense, I had been trans-ported, carried across to another time. Everywhere in this poem Lee demonstrates that kind of enchantment. On the August day when Lewis first saw the Missouri's source he wrote: "I had accomplished one of those great objects on which my mind was unalterably fixed for many years." The success of this poem must have given Lee a comparable emotion, and for good reason. Through his imaginative gift he gives all of us a chance to drink of that "tonic of wildness" without which, Thoreau said, we could not exist as sane beings. It is no small gift.

Philip F. Gura
Boulder, 1978

Acknowledgments

Art has rarely flourished without patronage. Not historically, not now. Lest we forget the generosity of patrons, I wish to acknowledge the many people who have enabled my husband, through his poem of Lewis and Clark, to chant into life the wonders of the West.

Roland C. Rautenstraus, President, University
    of Colorado
J. Russell Nelson, Chancellor, University of Colorado
William E. Briggs, Dean, College of Arts and Sciences
Milton E. Lipetz, Vice Chancellor for Research and
    Dean of the Graduate School
Dwight V. Roberts, President, University of
    Colorado Foundation, Inc.
The Allocations Committee, University of Colorado
    Foundation, Inc.

Jeanne Lee

Preface

*T*he Lewis and Clark expedition began with the philosophic curiosity of President Jefferson to explore the Western country—by boat, to explore and map and describe the entire length of the Missouri River to its source in the Rocky Mountains, and then to portage across to the headwaters of the Columbia River and down its myriad waters to the Pacific Ocean; in short, to discover the mythic Passage to India.

Jefferson laid secret plans for the expedition in 1802 and then, early in 1803, almost in fantasy, purchased the Louisiana Territry from Napoleon—*purchased* history—and set in violent motion his surrogate self, his secretary of two years, young Meriwether Lewis.

Lewis, with the consent of Jefferson, offered to his old friend William Clark a captaincy and equal command of the expedition. Clark accepted at once, though indeed, when his commission finally filtered through the office of the Secretary of War, Clark had been named but a second lieutenant. Both men spent the rest of the year 1803 in planning, purchasing supplies, and recruiting the men. They worked their way by December to the mouth of the Missouri River some eighteen miles above St. Louis and set up winter quarters at Camp Dubois, where they waited on the seasons.

On May 14, 1804, the Corps of Discovery launched the boats into the Missouri. Because they were headed toward possibly hostile Indians, they were organized as a military force: two captains (a concept unparalleled in military history), four sergeants, one corporal, over two dozen privates. These were assisted by civilian boatmen (mostly French), the interpreter George Drewyer, and Clark's black servant York. They sailed, rowed, poled, pulled against the current in three boats: a long keelboat with twenty-two oars and two smaller pirogues or dugout canoes.

This first leg of the journey in the summer of 1804—the broad Missouri meanders through prairie country—was tedious and slow, but always dangerous. The men themselves were not as yet tightly military. The Indians were a constant threat of catastrophe, especially the Teton Sioux. The river shrank in autumn to shallow channels between sand bars. At last in November, 1600 miles out, the party reached the safety of the Mandan villages (in central North Dakota), where they waited on winter and the river ice.

In the Spring of 1805 the keelboat was sent back to St. Louis with some of the men. Six dugout canoes were built from cottonwood trees to replace the keelboat. Another interpreter was hired, Touissant Charbonneau, who brought along one of his wives and her infant son. The party, now numbering thirty-five, set out again in the eight boats on April 7, 1805.

They moved in a paradise of Spring, through a land of prairies and uplands, rich in game, strangely empty of Indians. But time was lost deciding which of two forks was in fact the Missouri and time was lost again in the difficult portage around the Great Falls. It was late July before they reached Three Forks. There they had anticipated meeting the Shoshone Indians to assist them over the mountains, but there were no Indians at all. They did not find the Shoshone—Sacajawea's relatives—until they had hauled their canoes virtually all the way to the Continental Divide. They had hoped to portage their canoes across to the head-waters of the Columbia, but these waters, the Lemhi River and the Salmon River, were impossibly turbulent.

They were forced to abandon their boats, purchase horses, and travel overland in September on the Lemhi Trail to Travelers Rest and on the Lolo Trail across the Bitterroot Mountains to the Clearwater River. In this difficult high country of snow and near starvation, the most terrible and difficult country of all, mere survival was sufficient heroism.

Once on the Clearwater, five new boats were built, and the party moved with comparative ease (though with little food) down the Clearwater to the Snake, down the Snake to the Columbia, through the Narrows and the Cascades of the Columbia and on to the Pacific Ocean by mid-November—"land's end"—by their reckoning a total distance of 4,162 miles.

The factual record of this heroic expedition comes from various documents, but primarily from the daily journals kept by Lewis and Clark (Reuben Gold Thwaites, ed., *Original Journals of the Lewis and Clark Expedition, 1804–1806.* New York: Dodd, Mead, & Company, 1904, 8 vols.). The imaginary dialogues presented here are an interpretation of those journals and follow them very closely in language, syntax, and facts with but one major exception: the rumored details of life in the Mandan villages, ascribed to Drewyer in the October 21, 1804 dialogue, were taken from the work of a later visitor to the villages, the artist George Catlin.

Journal entries used as such are in italics.

R.E.L.

May 27ᵗʰ Sunday 1804

LEWIS: The unknown voyage!
          Sunset, dark clouds and lightning.
          George Shannon with a deer.
          There is so much to see.

CLARK: And write. I hate to write.
          Let's drink instead.

LEWIS: He said—

CLARK: I know he said.
          Is he some god?

LEWIS: It's his imagination
          That we ride this mighty river
          To its mountain source
          And down the other side
                              the route to India.
          To find and name.
          The two of us to write—

CLARK: The wind rises.

LEWIS: So that what we do will be more than
What we are.
Put down that we are one week beyond St. Charles
And past the last white settlement on the Missouri.

CLARK: I should put down that we are one week out,
Tired, bug-bitten, usually wet,
Sometimes quarrelsome,
Uncertain in command
And settling for a drink.
Shall I write that for Jefferson?
Is that not history?

LEWIS: What we see, what we do, what we write
Is history.

CLARK: Not what we are?
Two men drinking?

10th. of June 1804

CLARK: More whiskey, York,
And then I'll write
our party in high Spirits
Captain, except for you.
What is it you withhold?

LEWIS: Perhaps it's York that bothers me.
Why did you bring your slave?

CLARK: My servant, Captain.
You have a dog as big.

LEWIS: You do not answer me.
Why, always, "Captain"?

CLARK: Because you are a captain
          And I am not.

LEWIS: In name, if not commission.
          Equal—

CLARK: But not.

LEWIS: It bothers you?

CLARK: Yes, Captain. Sir.
          What is it bothers you?

LEWIS: Ticks, mosquitoes, the hard rain,
          The men, perhaps.
          Should we be honest with each other?
          Collins—

CLARK: Still? Three weeks ago!
          You were away.
          Warner and Hall absent without leave.
          Their sentences remitted.
          But Collins—

LEWIS: You lashed Collins.

CLARK: Had him lashed, Captain.

LEWIS: Concurred and watched the fifty lashes on the
              naked back
          For disrespectful language.

CLARK: And in your absence, too.

LEWIS: Away on business for the expedition.

CLARK: Yes. And thus
          Did I command.

LEWIS: Oh, I see.

CLARK: The men enjoyed the punishment.

LEWIS: And so they would, whatever the offense.
         Did you?

CLARK: The rules and articles of war—

LEWIS: Frightened.

CLARK: Then, perhaps.

LEWIS: Now?

CLARK: Now, all's delight.

Camp Mouth of the Kansies
June 29th. 1804

LEWIS: The water's warm with summer.
         Birds sing.

         John Collins and Hugh Hall
         Are found guilty of drawing whiskey
         From the common store
         And getting drunk on duty.

         The water's blue and wide.
         The men toil against the current.
         The water sounds and sings.
         Captain Clark hunts on shore.

July 4th *Wednesday*

LEWIS: Sergeant, order a discharge from the bow piece
           In honor of the day of independence of the U. S.

FLOYD: Sir.

CLARK: Sergeant, order an extra gill of whiskey for the men
           In honor of the same.

FLOYD: Sir.

Camp New Island, July 12th *1804*

CLARK: Private Willard, stand.
           The court martial of the two commanding officers
           Does find you guilty of every part of the charge
           Of lying down and sleeping on your post.

LEWIS: Concur.

CLARK: This being a breach of rules and articles of war
           And tending to the probable destruction of the party,
           We do sentence you to receive one hundred lashes
           On the bare back, at four different times
           In equal proportion,
           Punishment to commence this evening at sunset
           And continue to be inflicted by the guard
           Every evening until completed.

LEWIS: Concur.

Camp White Catfish Nine Miles above the Platt River Monday the 23rd. of July 1804

LEWIS: Delight!
A strange word for you.

CLARK: I won't use it, then, except
In the sense of whiskey.

LEWIS: But you enjoy the voyage.

CLARK: *Ticks & Musquitors.*
We've got to get on.

LEWIS: Delight in the voyage!
Ticks and mosquitoes, the gnats,
Rattlesnakes.
The boils, the felons, dysentery.

CLARK: *One man verry sick, Struck with the sun.*
Jos. Fields got bit by a snake.

LEWIS: You write that and say—I'll find it—
pleasing deversity to the senery.
Or this:
a high handsome Prarie.
Wolves and the night alarums.
Who knows where the Indians might be?
the Otteaus and Panies.
I must confess to some anxiety
As to what more may lie ahead.
We move from the known—

CLARK: Therein is the delight.
Oh, yes, the goods were wet in the boats,
And the time we had like to have stove our boat,

And the way the river rose a foot a day,
And the banks near caved us in,
The wind all high and wrong,
The heat, the rain,
The men as bad and in need of
                    a little punishment.

LEWIS: No, here it is, the sunset
                    Guilded in the most butifull manner.

CLARK: Very well, I will restrict myself
To the most ordinary—
                    Deer, buffalow
                    Grapes and raspeberries
                    1 Turkey   Several Grous

LEWIS: Your delight—

CLARK: and fear—

LEWIS: till now unknown.

*July 30*th *Monday 1804*

LEWIS: The sun loiters in the river,
Now drowns in gold,
Turns black in night.

What lies beyond?

We must fix each place on maps
And give out names,
Measure and record
The very sun and night.

         A fair Still evening.

Councile Bluff
August 3ʳᵈ. Friday 1804

CLARK: Every man on his guard and ready for anything!

LEWIS: Captain, they are but six.

CLARK: Six here, how many in the brush?

LEWIS: They brought—watermelons.

CLARK: But not the rascal, Le Bartee. Where's he?
The signs are wrong.

LEWIS: What signs, Captain?

CLARK: Le Bartee's running off,
The beaver foot caught in the trap,
Just the foot!
The death of the white horse.
The burial mounds.
The signs are all of death.

LEWIS: Six near-naked men, Captain.
We're near fifty.

CLARK: We invade their land, Captain.
The signs—

LEWIS: Hush, Captain. Show no fear.
After breakfast we will rig an awning from the sail
And speak with them on the wishes of our
government.
They will be impressed by long speech.
They will respond to ceremony.

Captains Lewis & Clark holding a Council with the Indians

CLARK: They will be more impressed
          By a few shots from a gun.

LEWIS: Gifts, medals, certificates.
          Whiskey, perhaps.

CLARK: We'll be on guard.
          I fear this place.
          Le Bartee has lost himself on the endless plains.
          A sign for all of us.

LEWIS: *We ar ruge nor. We ar ruge nor.*

CLARK: What sign is that?

LEWIS: The Ottoe's name. The other's *Little Thief.*

CLARK: We'll be on guard!

August 4th. Satturday

LEWIS: And now?
          Admit, Captain, the Indians were harmless.

CLARK: All right, nothing.
          Indians and nothing more.
          But Le Bartee's still gone
          And now young Reed
          Who was to go back to find his knife
          Has not returned.

5th of August Sunday 1804

LEWIS: Reed?

CLARK: We have some reason to believe he has deserted.

6th August, Monday 1804

CLARK: Reed's not come yet. Nor Le Bartee.

LEWIS: We're fifty miles from that camp.

7th August Tuesday 1804

LEWIS: All right, despatch four men.

CLARK: Drewyer, Fields, Bratten, and Labieche,
With orders to bring Reed back
Or put him to his death.

8th August Wednesday 1804

CLARK: No Reed.

9th. August Thursday 1804

CLARK: No Reed, no Moses Reed.
           Moses has gone to the promised land.

10th. August Friday 1804

CLARK: No Reed.

LEWIS: This was your omen then.

11th. August Satturday 1804

CLARK: No Moses B-for-Bastard Reed.

12th. August, Sunday 1804

CLARK: The wolf barks like a dog.

LEWIS: Another omen, I suppose, for Reed.

CLARK: Or Indians ahead.

13ᵗʰ August Monday 1804

LEWIS: We'll send five men to the Mahar town
          And wait in camp.

CLARK: Reed, Le Bartee, the four, now five more.
          What if the Indians attack?

14ᵗʰ August Tuesday 1804

CLARK: No Reed, no no one.

LEWIS: Send another man.

August 15ᵗʰ, Wednesday, 1804
Camp three Miles N. E.
of the Mahar Village

CLARK: No one.

16ᵗʰ August Thursday 1804
Fishing Camp 3 Mˢ N. E. of the Mahars

CLARK: None.

17ᵗʰ. *August Friday 1804*

LEWIS: So much for omens.
Reed, Labieche, Drewyer and party all are back
But Le Bartee, and he deceived them and is gone for
   good.
Nine Indians arrived.
My birthday will be a happy one.

CLARK: We'll shoot Reed thirty times to celebrate.

18ᵗʰ. *August, Sat'day 1804*

LEWIS: Reed's blooded thoroughly
By his own men and watched by Indians.

CLARK: Too easy, sir. The gantlet's less than death.

LEWIS: He's to be shunned as well,
Set quite apart, alone, a form of death.

CLARK: So much for Reed.
Come, the men dance.

19ᵗʰ. *August Sunday 1804*

CLARK: Oh, sir, the omens weren't for Reed but Sergeant
   Floyd.
He's sick to death.

20th. August Monday 1804

CLARK: He said to me, "I am going away."

LEWIS: We each voyage there,
Floyd, the white horse, and ourselves.

CLARK: *after paying all the honor*
to our Deceased brother
we camped in the Mouth of floyds River
a butifull evening.

14th. Sep^t. Friday 1804

CLARK: Captain, permission to walk today.

LEWIS: With York? the French boy? or alone?

CLARK: Alone.

LEWIS: Alone and not afraid, this dark and drizzly day.
Why? if I may ask, where there is much to fear.

CLARK: I am too much engaged in writing.

LEWIS: No answer, that. Perhaps, like Shannon,
You'll be gone some sixteen days, return,
Half-crazed.

CLARK: The man had liked to starve to death in a land of
plenty.
Buffalo, beaver, elk, deer, foxes,
Squirrels, rabbits, wolves, and goats.
No, I go to kill a goat.

LEWIS: Captain, it is an antelope. Not goat.

CLARK: You know no more than I.
           The beast is keenly made. It is a goat.
           To find the old volcano, then, the one McKey
               described.
           No, just to get away. Why else?

LEWIS: I would not lose you, Captain, on the naked plain.
           The Indians—

CLARK: To walk through Eden, safe with death.

LEWIS: In the dark rain.

CLARK: My self.

Monday September 17*th*. 1804

LEWIS: I saw today immense herds of buffalo.
           I should say three thousand.

CLARK: The plovers take their flight southerly.
           The days pass, Captain.

LEWIS: We still go north.

CLARK: The river shrinks to sand bars.

LEWIS: To the Teton Sioux.
           Are you not afraid?

CLARK: I am. Are you?

19th. of September Wednesday 1804

CLARK: Today I killed a elk.
York killed a buck.
The crew in the boat killed
Two buffalo in the river.
The hunters on shore also killed
Four deer with black tails.

Plums and grapes
And barking squirrels.

That creek I'll call Elm
And this one, Night.

28th. of September 1804 Friday

CLARK: I am very unwell for want of sleep.

LEWIS: Write that down, too, and drink.

CLARK: *I am verry unwell for want of Sleep.*
       Deturmined to Sleep tonight
The Indians! What are they?
We were near death.
Had you given the word to fire—

LEWIS: Had you fired—

CLARK: I did not expect—

LEWIS: We did expect, were ready.
       Here, drink.
We did succeed with feints alone. They lost.

CLARK: It was my fault, Captain. I wrote that.
           I felt My self Compeled to Draw my Sword.
           I felt My self warm & Spoke
           In verry positive terms.

LEWIS: Honest enough. You could not write down
           All the oaths you said.

CLARK: I could not write down the fear.
           They held my boat.
           They said that I should not go on.
           Drunk, assuming so, sucking the bottle for more,
           The one they call The Partisan came
           Staggering up to me and said—
           I know not what.

LEWIS: So much for our interpreters.
           It was my fault, the speech,
           On and on as usual, and they knew not a word.
           Though they knew your sword.
           You were right to name the place Bad Humor.

CLARK: That day was Tuesday.
           I have not slept since.

LEWIS: Drink, then.

CLARK: You had no fear. Next day you went on shore again
           And stayed three hours till I feared for you and came.

LEWIS: Treated like a king. Carried on a robe.

CLARK: Buffalo, highly decorated. There, seventy men.
           The pipe of peace. Peace!
           The down of swans. The dirty flags of Spain.

LEWIS: And our flag too.

CLARK: And sacrificed dog's balls to it.

LEWIS: In great solemnity.

CLARK: Danced half the night, the women.

LEWIS: The men beating on the tambourin.

CLARK: False! Deceptions! They would not let us pass!
           I could not sleep!

LEWIS: We were on guard, we were ready.
           Who would have guessed that night,
           The accident with the boat, my ordering the men
           With loud voice would frighten them?

CLARK: The night lined suddenly with two hundred men.
           All night some watched and waited. Who could sleep?

LEWIS: And let us pass today because
           You trained the swivel on the soldiers of the chief.

CLARK: Waiting for you to order me to fire.
           Oh death, would you have said?

LEWIS: I was that near.

CLARK: To massacre, of us and them.

LEWIS: Here, drink. So much for death.
           We routed them, they let us go.
           Thanks to your warm words.
           You realize what we've done,
           The river's free,
           The fur trade's clear.

CLARK: Here's history.
                          In my fear.

LEWIS: And, I confess, in mine.
           Drink. Sleep.

CLARK: *Deturmined to Sleep to night if possible.*

7th. of October Sunday 1804

CLARK: The Tetons follow still.
           The Indians!
           The Rikaras are next.
           The wind is hard ahead,
           Black clouds fly.
           There's frost
           And the track of a white bear.
           All on guard!

13th. of October Satturday 1804

CLARK: Fix your signature, Captain.

LEWIS: I hesitate.
           Shall a man be lashed and banned
           For his fear?

CLARK: But he was mutinous.
           They say he urged the men to leave us and return.

LEWIS: Is he not young?

CLARK: John Newman young? He's strong enough.
           These lashes are a paddling and no more.

LEWIS: Banned, assigned to drudgeries, to slops,
And then sent back—

CLARK: Mutinous, then, in his fear.

LEWIS: The way we all are with our gods.

CLARK: This is no time, then, to be weak.
Sign.
The men themselves condemned.

LEWIS: The men themselves are Indians.

CLARK: Are men, as thee.
Therefore sign.

LEWIS: Sign and the words will lash
John Newman to the end of history.

17th of October Wednesday 1804

LEWIS: Is it you? What time is it? What's the noise?

CLARK: Two squaws, Captain.
They sing and make merry.

LEWIS: The guard?

CLARK: Awake. On duty, more or less.
The squaws caress them
Now that York's passed out.

An American having struck a Bear but not killed him, escapes into a Tree

LEWIS: The Indians! What are they?
Those before would kill for rum.
These offer us their wives
But will not drink.
The squaws?

CLARK: Poor and filthy.
But we've been gone five months.

LEWIS: Two squaws in their civilities.

CLARK: They're young, Captain.
Two young squaws.
Five months, Captain.
Therefore come.

21st. October Sunday 1804

LEWIS: There will be much to write.

CLARK: Much to leave out.

LEWIS: Drewyer must be telling tales.

CLARK: The Indians! Use the glass.
See the women on the bank.

LEWIS: They are handsome, light.

CLARK: Naked under those robes. Whores.
Drewyer says that's why the traders
Winter here.
Our men are heated by his words.

LEWIS: Our men will have enough to do
            To build a fort. Winter will cool them.

CLARK: Look there, the boys, dressed like dandies.
            The sticks they carry, red-tipped.
            Drewyer says they symbolize their sex.
            He says too we will see men
            Dressed in squaw clothes.

LEWIS: Drewyer—

CLARK: He says they do a dance
            To bring in buffalo
            By the sound of rutting.

LEWIS: Write tonight that the ground
            Is covered with snow.
            Leave out the rest.
            Cloudy and cold.
            The snow falling,
            The land hostile, chill.
            We have come so far—

6th. November Tuesday 1804
Fort Mandan

CLARK: *last night late we were awoke*
                                by the Sergeant of the Guard
                                to see a Nothern light.

                                light
                                a great Space

8*th*. December Satturday 1804

CLARK: It was today twelve degrees below the naught.

LEWIS: And two suns in the misty sky.

CLARK: York frosted his penis.

LEWIS: Don't write that.

CLARK: I already have.

Fort Mandan on the NE Bank of the Missouries 1600 Miles up Tuesday January the 1*st*. 1805

CLARK:
The Day was ushered in
by the Descharge of two Cannon,
We suffered 16 men with their Musick
*to visit the 1*st*. Village*
for the purpose of Danceing.

5*th*. of January Satturday 1805

CLARK:
We sent a man to this Medisan Dance last night,
they gave him 4 Girls

12th. February Tuesday 1805

LEWIS: When you were on the hunt
          John Howard, back from some squaw, late,
          Rather than call the guard, scaled the wall.
          It was a breach of safety,
          So I summoned him to court—

CLARK: Captain?

LEWIS: —and then withheld the sentence.
          Enough of punishment for sins.
          We must try some other way
          To hold the men to our authority.

CLARK: A little punishment—

LEWIS: I'm in command.

CLARK: And so I see.
                    What other news?

LEWIS: Nothing important, but
          Jessaume and I helped deliver a child
          For the wife of Charbonneau,
          Her labor tedious, the pain intense.
          To hasten birth, we used dust
          Ground from the rattle of a rattlesnake.
          The babe arrived soon after, a fine boy.
          I question if the rattle dust did cause in fact—

CLARK: They say she is sixteen.
          Sah-kah-gar-we-a.

April the 2nd 1805

CLARK: Captain, it's time to load the boats.

LEWIS: I'll worry for the goods that must go back.
The men discharged are something less
Than those who will go on.

CLARK: John Newman pleads still to go on.

LEWIS: No, he goes back with Reed.
We must not swerve our word.

CLARK: And trust them, then?

LEWIS: With all the articles, you mean.
Animal skins and skeletons,
Maps and reports,
Sixty specimens of plants,
Four horns of the mountain ram,
The Mandan buffalo robe,
Yes, and the live magpies,
Burrowing squirrel and prairie hen.
What will become of them?
These are in some terrible way
More precious than the men.

CLARK: I'd not say that.

LEWIS: The journals even more.

CLARK: The voyage, the winter's sleep—

LEWIS: What lies ahead?
I wake at night,
The wild geese cry
Secrets of the dark.
My heart—

CLARK: Captain?

LEWIS: Do not the men—

CLARK: All the party is in high spirits.
They've no complaint except venereals.
All anxious to proceed.

LEWIS: With Charbonneau, his squaw and babe.
Imagine such a dangerous voyage
Accompanied by this squaw and babe.

CLARK: I'd not go back.

LEWIS: Nor I.
Yet we go to the dark.

CLARK: We must go on.

LEWIS: Yes, but to what?

CLARK: Shall I order the men
To load the boats?

LEWIS: Yes, of course.
I did not mean to hesitate.

Thursday April 18th. 1805

LEWIS: The boats leap in the wind.
The sky shows blue in the water.
I hear the old field lark sing.

The prairies green
And the geese feed
On the young grass.

White cranes rise
From the blue river.

The captain walks on shore
With Charbonneau, the squaw,
And the babe by the willows.

Now in our passage
The thousand geese rise.
All sound, all sight,
Waits on the beating of their wings,
Waits on their cries,
Till they are free from earth
All strung out in the sky.

Thursday May 9th. 1805

CLARK: Captain, I'll walk on shore
         And hunt until the wind comes.
         What would you like to eat tonight?
         Marrow bone?
         Beaver tail?

LEWIS: Buffalo, for the *poudinge blanc.*
         Let Charbonneau make a feast tonight.

CLARK: In exchange, sit at your desk
         And record just what it is.

LEWIS: A delicacy, Captain. A sausage.

CLARK: Record, then, how Charbonneau makes love
         To the gut with his forefinger and his thumb—

LEWIS: Gently compresses it until the—

CLARK: The shit, Captain.
         Be honest when you write.

LEWIS: The President's too fastidious—

CLARK: The west is not.
         The President would not invite you to his table now,
         All beard and stench, grime and rancid skins,
         Nor would he sit at ours
         To drink grog and eat the *poudinge blanc.*
         Be honest when you write.

LEWIS: He is a man that dreams.

CLARK: Give him ten days in steady wind
         And the ice forming on the oars.
         See if he dreams then.

LEWIS: And the game we slaughter,
         The buffalo for his tongue alone,
         Or the gut.

CLARK: Write true to the *pudinge blanc.*

14*th*. of May Tuesday 1805

CLARK: Drink, Captain, while you write.

LEWIS: I cannot but with horror recollect.

CLARK: We should never both be off the boats.

LEWIS: Three hundred yards away, to watch the wind
         Catch her sail and overturn—

CLARK: Charbonneau should have put the boat before the
              wind
          Instead of luffing her.
          And then the bastard stood there
          And cried to God for mercy.

LEWIS: Cruzatte threatened to shoot him then and there.

CLARK: Till he took hold of the rudder.

LEWIS: I nearly tried to swim across,
          The boat thus on its side,
          My life then nothing if the medicines
          And instruments and books were gone.

CLARK: Cruzatte saved her, cutting the sail.

LEWIS: Swamped with water.

CLARK: Did you see the squaw calmly
          Catch the articles that floated out?

LEWIS: All's wet.

CLARK: But saved.

LEWIS: We'll camp tomorrow and dry the goods
          And then go on.

May 19ᵗʰ. Sunday 1805

CLARK: *after killing the Bear*
                          I continued my walk alone,
                          & killed 3 Deer & a Beaver
                          finding that the Perogues were below

I assended the highest hill I could see,
from the top of which I saw the mouth
of M. Shell R
& the meanderings of the Missouri
for a long distance.
I also saw a high mountain
in a westerly direction.

Sunday May 26th. 1805

LEWIS:

these points of the Rocky Mountains
were covered with snow
and the sun shone on it
in such a manner as to give me
the most plain and satisfactory view.
while I viewed these mountains
I felt a secret pleasure
in finding myself so near the head
of the heretofore conceived boundless
Missouri.

Friday May 31st. 1805

CLARK: I make it eighteen miles today.
Eighteen hard—what is this?
ruins of eligant buildings
collumns
pedestals and capitals

LEWIS: The cliffs today. As I say,
with the help of a little immagination

CLARK: A little! They are rocks only.

LEWIS: *seens of visionary enchantment*

CLARK: Oh, Captain, instead put in the mud along the bank,
          The men pulling the damn boats in cold water
          Up to their armpits all the day.
          Put in that the water is swift,
          That the men's feet are raw.
          Write down that the game is scarce,
          That the land's a desert.
          Write that the air's so dry
          The inkstand's dried up.
          Don't write me
                    seens of visionary enchantment
          When the supply of liquor is running low.

LEWIS: You are not moved—
          Oh—it is a joke.

CLARK: Captain, I have offended you.

LEWIS: Oh, no.
          Yet I thought—
          It will seem strange if I—
                    and you,
          If the two journals—

CLARK: I shall, if you like, mention buildings.

LEWIS: History is also what we feel.

CLARK: You seldom—

LEWIS: Please.

CLARK: I shall say
                    romantick
          But no more.

*Sunday June 9*th. *1805*

CLARK: The men all say that you and I are wrong.
           They dance and sing songs to his violin
           And Cruzatte has their confidence
           And Cruzatte says that the right fork
           Is the Missouri and not the left.

LEWIS: The men do not cogitate
           As we have done for seven days.
           Did we not independently arrive
           At the same conclusion?

CLARK: The left fork is clear,
           The right is muddy.
           If we are wrong—

LEWIS: The men know only what they see.
           They do not think.

CLARK: We're not above them.

LEWIS: We're in command
           And the men are cheerful.

CLARK: The right fork—

LEWIS: Will henceforth, with your permission,
           Be called Maria's.

CLARK: Oh, I see.

LEWIS: You will recall your Judith
           And the river named for the Indian squaw.

CLARK: I do not object, of course,
           But such a turbulent and troubled water?

LEWIS: Maria's is a noble river.
           The river bottoms form one immense garden
           Of roses, now in full blow.
           The bird songs are wild and simple, gay,
           Sung most enchantingly.

CLARK: And therefore, I suppose, could not be
           The masculine Missouri.
           Go, Captain, dance with Cruzatte
           And tell him how you cogitate.
           Ah, no matter.
           The men are drilled somehow to follow us
           Without the threat of punishment.
           Cruzatte is wrong.

LEWIS: The river's name: Maria's.

Sunday June 16th 1805

CLARK: The men now know Cruzatte was wrong
           But wish they paddled wrong
           In that sweet stream
           Rather than face
           This great falls.

LEWIS: Who would have thought them
           So romantic?

CLARK: They find omens
           In the bears, in the eagle's nest,
           In the innumerable rattlesnakes
           And most of all
           In the condition of the squaw.
           She is extremely ill.
           Her case is dangerous.
           She lies near death.

LEWIS: So do we all.
           So are we all at times
           Low-spirited.
           Yet we've not come this far
           To die.

CLARK: The great falls are terrible
           To contemplate.

LEWIS: They are sublime.
           Magnificent and sublime.

CLARK: Impassable, as death.

LEWIS: We'll find a way around,
           Find trees, make wheels,
           And portage all the boats.
           This is a place where we'll survive
           Through our belief.
           We must get on.

Thursday July 4th*. 1805*

LEWIS: Sergeant, a gill of whiskey for the men
           In honor of the day of independence of the U. S.

CLARK: A year has passed; in all,
           A year and a month and a week.
           An extra gill for ourselves, Captain.
           Drink while you can,
           It is the last of the spirits.

LEWIS: Now, Captain, we've come this far.
           The men dance and sing.

The bears and buffaloes
As the stars
Hear the sweet music
Of this night.

CLARK: Your cheerfulness rings somewhat false.
We enter—what did you write—
the most perilous and difficult part
of our voyage.

LEWIS: Will you cry omens again? Why repine?
The squaw survived,
The boats and all supplies are wheeled
These twenty miles around the falls.
The iron boat waits only to be pitched.
We dance and drink and eat
a very comfortable dinner
of bacon, beans, suit dumplings
& buffaloe beaf

CLARK: You make it sound a game of children.

LEWIS: The canoe on wheels, the sail hoisted,
The party blown merrily by the wind across the plains.

CLARK: Wind, wind every day. A most dreadful wind.
Storms. The hail so violent the men
Were knocked down and blooded frightfully.

LEWIS: The sight of ten thousand buffalo!
Who has seen to record such a sight?

CLARK: I mind the time you shot a buffalo
And watched the blood gush in streams
From his mouth and nostrils—
And, your gun unloaded,
Were stalked by a bear.

LEWIS: That day was like a dream,
Much like the day
The buffalo calf followed after me
As would my dog.

CLARK: But remember when you woke and found
The rattlesnake ten feet away?

LEWIS: What is your point, Captain?
I grant you it's no game.

CLARK: It is—
I don't know what it is.
I want somehow to
Chisel my name on a rock
With the date.
But that's vanity.
I want—
Oh, I am anxious to get on
And don't know why.

LEWIS: It is, as I shall name my leather boat,
"Experiment," perilous and difficult.
Drink to that.

CLARK: Drink fast.
Here comes another shower of rain.
To stop the dancing of the men.

*Wednesday July 24*th. *1805*

LEWIS: To port, hills falling off to arid plain.
Starboard, hills rising; and beyond,
Dark and purple mountains
Ranged one above the other
To the lofty peaks of snow.

Captain Clark and his men shooting Bears.

Winds, mysterious noise,
The haunts of savages
                    unknown.
Day after day, mile after mile
They lie in watch,
                    the mountains.
We move slowly closer,
                    perilous.
Presently we'll turn
To assault the peaks.

Sunday July 28th. 1805

LEWIS: You walked twelve days.

CLARK: For all the good of it.
            Where are the Indians?

LEWIS: Vanished, to the mountains.
            The squaw knows this place,
            Though she shows no emotion
            Of sorrow or of joy.
            Give her enough to eat
            And a few trinkets
            And she will be content anywhere.
            Home, to us—

CLARK: This is my home, this bower
            Where you have forced me to rest.

LEWIS: Your feet all blisters, blood, pus, and scabs.
            Your bowels?

CLARK: Five Rush's pills have operated well.
            I'm ready once again.

LEWIS: Then you will ride the boats.
I'll walk ahead.
There is no argument.

CLARK: And how long will we float on this?
Here at the mouth it's ninety yards,
But see the mountains there, how close,
How high. It's not the Missouri now.

LEWIS: With your permission, three noble streams.
There's Madison's, there's Gallatin,
This we shall call the Jefferson.
This is a momentous day.

August 9ᵗʰ. Friday 1805

CLARK: He walks to save me,
Yet reports he has lost a tomahawk
And Shannon once again
And left a note for me
On a green pole
Which a beaver ate.
    And named two stinking creeks
    Wisdom and Philanthropy.
I should have made the trip
But for the fury
Of this tumor.
Let him blow the trumpet
For Shannon
And be the first to
Wade the river.
He came back, I think,
To tell me that, excited,
As a child.

Sunday August 11ᵗʰ. 1805

LEWIS: Damn you, Shields!
The Indian's whipped his horse and fled.
Why did you press on so and frighten him?
The first we've seen!
What did you think I waved the blanket for
And held up trinkets for
And then stripped up my shirt
To show the color of my skin?
Our very lives depend on them!
Where is my spy glass?
You've left it?
Damn you, Shields!

August 12ᵗʰ. Monday 1805

CLARK: *the river much more Sholey than below*
which obliges us to haul the Canoes
over those Sholes
men much fatigued and weakened
men complain verry much
I passify them.

Why this travail?
When will the mountains end?
The captain's on ahead. How far?
How much longer?

Monday August 12ᵗʰ. 1805

LEWIS: There

                    McNeal exultingly stood
                    with a foot on each side
                    and thanked his god
                    that he had lived to bestride
                    the mighty & heretofore deemed endless
                    Missouri.

        And here

                    I first tasted the water
                    of the great
                    Columbia.

Saturday August 17ᵗʰ. 1805

LEWIS: They have among them four hundred horses—
                    you're in good health again?
They were afraid I lured them to their death.
Nothing would convince them. I lied to them.
I slept but little.
I gave my cocked hat to the chief.
I am myself metamorphosed into an Indian.
See how they study York.
Imagine! the squaw the sister of the chief.
The river—I drank from the water of the Columbia!
I have tasted salmon!
So many toilsome days and restless nights.
They are, I cannot understand, human and brute.
You did not see them tear at the raw meat,
Pitifully hungry, gracious, kind.

The men must give a trinket
And ask permission of the husband.
They have the venereal
And I deduce it is a native disorder.
They danced all night.
Sixty horsemen came riding down on us
To rescue the old woman and the girl.
I'd painted vermillion on her face
And shouted *tab-ba-bone*
And—I'm afraid I upbraided Shields—
Finally they all caressed and hugged me
Till I was besmeared with their grease and paint
And heartily tired of their national hug.
Their chief is *Came-ah-wait.*

CLARK: What lies beyond?

LEWIS: Immense ranges of high mountains still to the west.

CLARK: The water route?

LEWIS: They say impassable,
But it must not be.

Sunday August 18^{*th*}*. 1805*

LEWIS: He leaves me
To gloom my birthday out alone
And make vain resolutions
Concerning time.
He shames my indolence
And selfishness.

Would that my time
In this sublunary world
Be but half complete!
Yet nothing's done.
I live shrouded, alone,
In my own dark thoughts.
Worthless, but to barter horses.
West is north.
It rains.

August 24th. Satturday 1805

CLARK: Colter will take back this word:
        The river route's impassable.
        The water's confined between huge rocks,
        And the current beats, foaming and roaring,
        From one to the other.
        Buy more horses. We must cross the peaks.
        It's cold.

September 4th. Wednesday 1805

CLARK: September. Snow.
        The worst roads that ever horses passed.
        Little to eat and the men hourly complaining
        Of their wretched situation.

LEWIS: The Indian says we shall soon reach
        The Flathead village
        Where we can buy more horses
        And trade off the poor ones.

CLARK: Nine pheasants for the entire party,
Berries, the flour nearly out
And but little corn.

LEWIS: He says we shall be in a valley then
And out of these rugged hills.
Do you despair, Captain, like the men?

CLARK: No, but I take this opportunity,
Like the men, to complain.
This is one damn steep rocky—
Who ever thought the Missouri
And the Columbia
Could be joined by portage?

LEWIS: It was a hope, now gone,
A reason for our being here.
Perhaps we have no reason now.
When I found it folly
To think of attempting to descend
That river in canoes,
I directed the fiddle to be played,
Lest the men know the state of my own mind.

CLARK: You are secret, Captain.
I am wet and frozen
And thirsty for a drink.

Wednesday 18^{*th*}*. Sept*^{*r*}*. 1805*

LEWIS: Back there, the Shoshone, remember,
With nine feet of deer guts, chewing on one end
And squeezing the contents out the other.
I said he was a brute—we are no better.
We've killed our colts and eaten them
And thought them fine meat—I am no better.

CLARK: The men are hungry still and much fatigued.
         We must do something to revive their spirits.

LEWIS: Mountains in every direction
         As far as the eye can see.
         Snow, deep snow.
         Lost, lost in the snow.

CLARK: Do you complain, Captain?

LEWIS: Here, it is as if there were
             nothing upon earth
                 except ourselves
         And we are brute creation
         With no more meaning than the birds.

CLARK: Do you despair, Captain?

LEWIS: Here's history:
         Cold, hungry, lost.
         Crows and ravens.

CLARK: This will end,
         The mountains end,
         They'll fall away.
         The guide says there's a prairie near.

LEWIS: The guide's a fool.

CLARK: Let me rush hunters on ahead
         To the promised plain, find game
         And send it back to cheer the men.

LEWIS: Leave me alone again.

CLARK: Captain?

LEWIS: Even the babe sucks on a bone.

Tuesday 24th*. Sept*^{r}*. 1805*

CLARK: Captain, try to mount the horse.
It is a gentle one.
We must go on.

LEWIS: I think that I have come to this fair plain to die.

CLARK: It is the sudden food—the roots and salmon.
If you would puke—take Rush's pills,
Try jalap, salts, tartar emetic, try anything.

LEWIS: I cannot even crawl.

CLARK: Oh, Captain, try to mount the horse.
You said, you wrote that we had triumphed,
That was your word, triumphed.

LEWIS: Triumph! I was wrong.

CLARK: Over the rocky mountains—
The ocean lies ahead—
We must go on.

LEWIS: Leave me, please.

CLARK: Captain, mount the horse.

October 6th*. Sunday 1805*

LEWIS: What country's this?
What is that noise?

CLARK: The men finish the canoes.
        We leave tomorrow
        For the ocean.

LEWIS: There is no ocean, none.
            I would fly.

CLARK: We are but men.

LEWIS: Beware the squaws.
        Venereal makes them stink.

CLARK: It is the fish.

LEWIS: Give me a fish
        Lest I eat my own bowels.
        Poudinge blanc.

CLARK: Soup, made from a horse.

LEWIS: The pain!
        I will stay here
        And dig roots.

CLARK: Captain, you've been sick two weeks.
        We must get on.
        The winter comes.

LEWIS: Leave me here.
        I am Shannon, lost.
        This is a fair country.
        Leave me.

October 9ᵗʰ. Wednesday 1805

LEWIS: What is that noise?

CLARK: One of the squaws who follow us.
I will go see.

LEWIS: She shrieks, she cries, she sings.
I have heard such voices in the night,
Like water—the music of hard water.
I have wished to sing like that.
Perhaps I have.

CLARK: A dreadful sight. She has a crazy fit.
With flint she's cut her arms
From wrists to shoulders.
The blood flies out
In her dance.

LEWIS: Pitied by all, she sang.
Did I—

CLARK: You were very sick, Captain,
But recovering fast.

LEWIS: I dreamed we were in water.

CLARK: True, Captain. The canoes were made and launched.
We head down river to the Snake
And down the Snake to the Columbia
And then—the ocean.

LEWIS: I remember.

CLARK: Rapids and riffles delayed us.
Gass's canoe overturned.
The men who could not swim
Clung desperately to a rock.
The goods were soaked.
You did not know, I think.

LEWIS: Cradled, like a babe.
And did I—sing?

CLARK: Strange talk, perhaps.

LEWIS: And you?

CLARK: I took command.
          Yet—

LEWIS: Listen. She cries again.

CLARK: —missed you.

Octr 10th. 1805 Thursday

LEWIS: This is very strange,
          These close clouds,
          The barren hills,
          The peaceable Indians
          Who watch us pass
          On the water.

          White, green, and light blue,
          Sea shells and curious bones,
          Otter skins and quilled brass.

CLARK: Stranger still to eat their dogs.

LEWIS: Dog's-flesh is ours.

CLARK: What, Captain?

LEWIS: Nothing.

A Canoe striking on a Tree.

October 17ᵗʰ Thursday 1805

CLARK: There is so much to write!
The great Columbia at this junction
Measures eight hundred and sixty yards across.

LEWIS: Yes, oh yes, did he not say
To seek the most direct and practicable
Water communication across the continent,
And have we not done so?

CLARK: Two hundred of the Sukulk tribe
Came singing and beating on their drums.

LEWIS: He said the object of the mission
Was the direct water communication
From sea to sea.

CLARK: They circled us and beat the drums
And sang—it was a famous day.

LEWIS: He said, in his instructions,
That we were, somehow, to strengthen
The authority
      of reason and justice.
Reason and justice!
In such a land!

CLARK: We smoked with them
And gave them medals
And the speech.

LEWIS: And purchased eight dogs to eat.

October 18ᵗʰ. Friday 1805

LEWIS: Beads, bells, and thimbles
Bought forty dogs.
The place is bedlam.
Write that.

CLARK: We're ready, Captain, to depart.

LEWIS: He said, I heard him,
The journey's merely literary,
To inform.

CLARK: I'll give the order.

LEWIS: Fatigues, dangers, honors,
Reason, justice,
Such as they are.

CLARK: Though late departing,
We should make twenty miles today.

October 19ᵗʰ. Saturday 1805

CLARK: This was strange: they were much frightened.
Thirty-two men, women, and children
Had crowded into the one lodge.
They cried, they wrung their hands,
Some hung down their heads,
Until I gave my hand to them all.
Yet, had I wished, I could have
Tomahawked them one by one.

LEWIS: And did you wish?

CLARK: You see, waiting there on the rock,
        I'd shot a crane.
        They'd never heard a gun
        And saw the bird fall.
        Confused, they said we came
        From the clouds
                and were not men.

LEWIS: But gods.

CLARK: The women's breasts are large
        And hang down very low.

LEWIS: Write that.

October 20*th*. Sunday 1805

LEWIS: Write that today we saw an Indian
        In a sailor's jacket.

CLARK: And some in scarlet or blue cloth robes.

LEWIS: Record the pelicans and black cormorants
        The speckled gulls and the blue teal.

CLARK: I shall write about the burial vault
        Sixty feet in length, with piles of great numbers
        Of human bones of every description.

LEWIS: Twenty-one skulls in a circle.

CLARK: And the skeletons of horses.

LEWIS: And our deaths, too.

CLARK: Captain?

LEWIS: Nothing.

CLARK: We made forty-two miles today.
             The flavor of the ducks, delicious.

October 21st. Monday 1805

CLARK: Taste this.
             You see, Captain, a week ago
             John Collins corked up
             Some wet and mouldy quarmash bread.
             It's soured now and makes
             A beer.

LEWIS: With rapids more dangerous
             As each day goes by—a beer.
             Give Collins immortality in beer.
             We shall all die
             And be—not men.
             Beer and bones.

CLARK: Drink, my captain.
             The wind is cold.

October 26th. 1805 Saturday

LEWIS: Hard rough black rock,
             The water swells and boils,
             But we have come through.

             Now in the calm morning
             Great numbers of white cranes.

Cruzatte plays his violin,
York dances for the chiefs,
The men strip naked in the sun
—to kill their fleas.

We are but men who die
And must acknowledge that
Before we try
—with the white cranes.

October 29th. Tuesday 1805

LEWIS: Sixteen dogs today.

CLARK: The chief showed me in his bag
            Fourteen cut-off fingers painted red.
            What are the Indians?

LEWIS: What are men?
                Vain, crawling things
                Shaped to the land.

CLARK: Write that to Jefferson.

LEWIS: He will read how pleased
            They were with music
            Of the violin.

October 31st. Thursday 1805

CLARK: Now is the last obstacle to our way,
            This great chute.

The water passes with great velocity
Foaming and boiling
In a most horrible manner.

LEWIS: We'll portage, like the Indians,
And destroy the obstacle.

CLARK: Beyond, just beyond,
The water's calm,
Responsive to the thrust and pull
Of tide.

November 3ʳᵈ. Sunday 1805

LEWIS: We have come through,
my friend, my good friend,
The last obstacle to our way.
But now the fog descends,
Great death-like fog.
Geese, brants and ducks,
Cranes and gulls,
Swans and storks
All wait
And make horrid noise.
The tide, the tide
Urges us on.

November 7ᵗʰ. Thursday 1805

CLARK: *Ocian in view! O! the joy.*

November 18th. Monday 1805

LEWIS
AND
CLARK:

We were most fooled in our joy.
And most miserably tired
By wind and rain.
Pinned down on a point of land,
Wet and cold,
Assailed by lightning and hail
And the full fury of the wind,
Immense waves for days on end,
Constant rain—
But it's over now
And the men behold
With great astonishment
The ocean.

Thursday November 21st. 1805

CLARK:

An old woman & Wife to a Cheif
of the Chunnooks
came and made a Camp near ours.
She brought with her
6 young Squars
(her daughters & nieces)
I believe for the purpose of
Gratifying the passions
of the men.

Saturday November 23rd. 1805

CLARK:

*A calm Cloudy morning,
a moderate rain the greater part
of the last night.*

*Capt. Lewis Branded a tree
with his name Date &c.*

*I marked my name
the Day & year
on a alder tree.*

Postscript

*T*he six charges of the Chinook woman—
"the old baud"—spread syphilis widely among the men,
as melancholic and anti-climactic as the trip back home
the following year.

The men spent four miserable rainy months at Fort
Clatsop near the mouth of the Columbia and de-
parted—"as in freedom won"—on March 23, 1806.
They worked their way slowly up river to the Cascades
and the Narrows, portaged, moved on to Celio Falls,
and eventually purchased from the Indians enough
horses to enable them to abandon their canoes and
move by land. They traveled faster than the seasons
and reached the Bitterroot Mountains when the snow
was still too deep for travel. They waited at Camp
Chopunnish from May 14 to June 10 and then tried
again. The dreadful mountains melted with the snow.
They reached Travelers Rest on June 30.

Here, still in search of the Passage to India, they
separated. Clark took half the party on nearly the same
route (but a shorter one) back to Three Forks, then over
Bozeman Pass to the Yellowstone River and down it by
canoe to its junction with the Missouri. He stopped
once to climb a landmark rock and carve his name. He
called the rock Pompey's Tower for Sacajawea's son.
The inscription—"Wm. Clark, July 25, 1806"—is still
visible, as if to say: I was here. This is now my country.

Lewis took his party east instead of south, travelling up the Blackfoot River, crossing the Divide, and going down the Sun River directly to Great Falls. Dividing his party (six went on down the Missouri by boat), Lewis and three others headed north by horseback to explore the area of the Marias River. It was on July 26 that they met up with eight Piegan Blackfoot Indians and on the next day that the Indians tried to steal their horses. Reuben Fields killed one Indian—"stabed the Indian to the heart with his knife"—and Lewis, that gentle man, another: "I shot him through the belly." The men hastily retreated to the Missouri, riding as much as a hundred miles in one day. They rejoined the other six men, turned their horses loose, and headed on by boat to rendezvous with Clark on August 12. But blood was shed again on August 11 when Cruzatte accidentally wounded Lewis in the left buttock. Lewis recorded it thus: "I instantly supposed that Cruzatte had shot me in mistake for an Elk as I was dressed in brown leather and he cannot see very well; under this impression I called out to him damn you, you have shot me."

Lewis spent most of the rest of the trip recuperating. The party reached the Mandan villages on August 14, passed the site of the Teton difficulty on August 26, reached Floyd's grave on September 4 (ten days to travel the space of 167 days, two years earlier), purchased whiskey from traders on September 6, and reached St. Charles on September 21. Clark's final journal entry was September 26: "a fine morning we commenced wrighting &c."

Clark lived to be sixty-eight and Governor of Missouri. Lewis became moody and alcoholic and died, either by murder or suicide, on the Natchez Trace at the age of thirty-five in 1809. Perhaps the best epitaph for both of the men is the strange toast Lewis gave at a banquet held in his honor in Washington on January 14, 1807: "May works be the test of patriotism as they ought, of right, to be of religion."

Captain Lewis shooting an Indian.